# Subject To

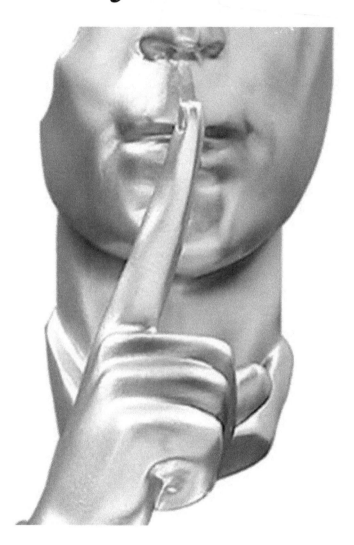

*Poetry by*
**Linda Clayton**

First paperback edition 2022

ISBNs:
Paperback: 978-1-80227-879-8
eBook: 978-1-80227-880-4

# Contents

# *Life*

# I Cannot See

I may not see the way you do,
With eyes so bright and quick,
I know that there are flowed about,
And where the grass grows thick.

I know that you are kind of little,
And I know that you're not tall,
I can see so many things,
That you cannot see at all.

I use my ears and hands for eyes,
And make them see for me,
I listen hard and gently touch,
And thus, it is I see.

God must have had a reason,
For making me like this,
Perhaps he meant for me to see,
What other people miss.

# The World May Never Notice

The world may never notice,
If the snowdrops do not bloom,
Or even pause to wonder,
If the petals fall too soon,
But every life that ever falls
Or ever comes to be,
Touches the world in some kind of way,
For all eternity.
The little one we longed for,
Was swiftly here and gone,
But the love that was then planted,
Has been and gone.
And although their arms were empty,
Our hearts knew what to do,
Every beating of my heart,
Said that I love you.

# The Way of Life

The way of life
It is full of rocks and hills
It is sometimes difficult to walk
Because we lose
Or simply chose the wrong path
Lord! For times in my life
Times that have no
I can see clearly
Seems like everything is dark,
I see nothing
Then seek the Lord thy light
I ask for your guidance
I need to drink from your fountain
The water of life
I need to feel your love
Your forgiveness to continue
My journey
I know that I love, feel, and live.
So, Father, give me encouragement
Give me strength and wisdom
So I can continue
Step by step
With your hand on me,
I know that I will do my walk
In love with the goodness of hope
In faith, in life!

# Struggling

You may have seen me struggling,
You may have seen me fall,
Regardless if I'm weak or not,
I'm going to stand tall.

Everybody thinks life is easy,
But the reality is it isn't at all,
People get hurt and struggle,
And are constantly put on the spot.

But I'm going to wear the biggest smile,
Whether I'm happy or not, destined to die,
And it's hard; I will find my way through,
So you may see me struggle,
But fall, I will not.

# A New Beginning

I will try to do my best and trust in you to do the rest,
I will try to keep my cool even if you're acting the fool,
I will try to remember why I couldn't just walk on by,
I will try to put you first
And not let your bubble burst.
I will try to keep my calm,
And not cause you any harm,
I will try to understand
And be proud to hold your hand.
Alone I'll try with all my heart to never ever let us part,
I'll try to work as part of the team,
And hold on to our dreams,
I will try to do what's right
And always love you with all my might.

# Too Fast

Have you ever watched arcades or the merry-go-round,
Listened to the rain falling on the ground,
Ever followed a butterfly with that endless flight?
If you haven't, slow down; you're going too fast.

Ever told your child you will do it tomorrow,
And in haste did not see his sorrow,
Ever lost touch and a good friendship has died,
Because you never had time to say, "Hi"?
You'd better slow down; you're going too fast.

Do you run through each day on the fly,
When you say, "How are you", do they reply,
When the day is done, do you lay in bed,
With the next hundred chores running through your head?
You'd better slow down; you're going too fast.

When you run so fast to get somewhere,
You missed half the fun of getting there,
When you worry and hurry through the day,
It's like an open gift that you've thrown away; life is not a race,
Slow down; you're going too fast.

# Nothingness

Out of the nothingness of sleep,
And soft dreams of eternity,
I came to you from over the deep blue sea,
I came to you because you called.
I had to fight through many stars,
Even into the place called Mars,
I was afraid, but you needed me.

Looking into your sleepy eyes,
There was no doubt at all you were mine.
I gave you ten kisses and a golden touch,
I floated up and down your body,
And you could feel each tender loving touch.
Our bodies were embracing,
You arched your back with mine,
It was the love that we were making.
It had been a long, long time,
In life, we had been lovers,
In death, we won't be apart,
For it is just my ghost that enters your body,
Oh yes, still lovers we are.

# The True Me

Don't believe my words,
The lies that I fabricate too,
To make you think I have a life,
To convince you I'm okay.
Don't trust the smile you see,
It's just put there; it isn't me.
Don't get fooled by my laughter,
It's merely an echo, a yearning,
For sorrow to return.
Please don't get convinced by my elder and order,
Born in an attempt to control the chaos,
And panic the storm brewing inside.
Don't be blinded by the perfection
Don't believe what you see,
It's not me!

# I Can Just Remember This

I didn't want to remember.
Children, shivering and shaking like the wind,
Mothers, searching for a piece of stale bread,
Shadows on thin legs moving with fear;
No, we didn't want to remember any of this,
Families that moved, vanished during the night,
Fleeing for their safety.

The mass graves, the smell of death, the smoke,
Pile the bodies and pile them high,
Make them a mountain up to the sky,
Toss them and turn them and keep them as well,
It will not hurt them, they're all going to hell.
The bodies are useless, the souls will be set free,
But stories are fixed in their glassy-grained eyes,
And we can still feel the pain that's hidden inside.

# The Tramp

He woke to the sound of the pigeon's call,
On a cold January day,
Covering his head as the snowflakes fell,
And wiped a tear away.

The day grew cold as dusk came near,
He had no food to eat,
So cold he couldn't feel the tears,
So cold he couldn't feel his feet.

A passer-by lifted his helpless head,
What's happened to you, my friend?
The tramp lay there dead,
Compassion was lost in the end.

# Not the Same as You

Do you know what I think,
Or how I really feel?
Do you wonder who I'll be,
Or if I'll ever heal?

Do you wonder if I love you,
Or if my life has any meaning?
Do you wonder if I know you
As another human being?

I wish I could answer all your questions
In a way you'd understand,
But all I have is mixed-up pieces,
That don't fit in any place.

All I ask is that you love me,
Even though blind faith is hard.
One day you'll have the answers –
It will be a great reward.

# Ignorance

Of human ignorance, I am almost in desperation.
For racism is around us everywhere,
But they say ignorance is bliss,
Just like Judas with a kiss.

So many people are still judged by their race.
This really shouldn't happen in this place,
Martin Luther King had the right things to say,
It's just a pity he's not here today.

So many holding the reins of power are not spiritually aware,
And racism is around everywhere,
And racism only leads to division and war.
Just goes to show how ignorant we all are.

# Teardrops

Today I saw a teardrop just resting on my sleeve,
He said his name was heartache,
And he came to watch me grieve.
He showed me many horrible things,
This drop of liquid pain,
I tried to wipe this tear away,
But it turned into a stain.
He said, "Look a little closer,
And tell me what you see,"
The more I looked, the more I tried
To rid this stain from me.
And another tear ran down my cheek,
My sleeve again wiped it away,
Then it started to speak to me,
"My name is past regret,"
And the things you've seen are true,
But as I peeped inside that tear,
All I could see was you.

# Autism

Here I am, living inside my own little world,
Do you think I don't listen? I hear every word.
Sometimes I get frustrated because you don't understand,
It's not my fault, it's the way I am.
I wish I could say what I shouldn't say,
But I'm autistic, and it gets in the way.
For those who don't know me,
They probably think I am out of control,
If only they could be in my role.
There are lots of others who feel like me,
We are not simple; we can talk,
But it's two steps forward, ten steps back,
Will they ever get the answer to that?
Families and friends try their best,
But they are exhausted
And in desperate need of a rest.
Someday I hope they will find a way,
To unlock that part of me.

# Thinking Back to When

Many, many years ago,
When I was just a kid,
And I had just begun to grow,
Well, maybe just a bit,
I'm thinking back on all those things,
That life saw fit to give me,
If I can't remember everything,
Please, I hope you will forgive me –
Chocolate, sweets, big bubble gum,
Mini rolls and Coca-Cola,
Saturday morning picture show,
Usherette who would bring ice cream,
And the film would finish up with
The National Anthem, 'God Save the Queen'.
In school, the teacher had to see,
Just what she had to do,
You had one finger up for a wee,
And two up for a poo.
Measles, mumps and Chickenpox
Always seemed to share,
They opened up Pandora's box,
And caught us unawares.
Well, medicine and care from Mum,
Our time in bed was done,
And whatever it was that we had wrong,
Didn't take long.

# Because

Because I know how cruel,
Just common words can be,
I thought the words were singing things,
With colours like the sea.
But since I've felt their caustic lash
And know how that can sting,
I hold my breath when words go by,
In case they will not sing.

# Dreams

They say we're living longer,
I wonder what that means.
Gives us more time to plan ahead,
And to relieve our dreams.
No, I don't see life like that, not when you're 92,
The best thing that could happen to me,
Is to forget to let me go through.
Look at these crumpled-up hands,
I can no longer sew or knit,
My eyes are dim, I cannot see,
But only just a bit.
My walking, it is very slow,
It doesn't get me where I want to go,
I have to stop and have a shit,
I just don't see the need of it.
It's all right for Jack; he's dead,
One night he was making love in bed,
He didn't think of me,
Selfish to the core, you see.
Come on, stop moaning,
Have another half; there's plenty more fish in the sea,
But you must look hard.
Anyway, if you had a man,
Whatever would you do?
I don't know, but I could show him a thing or two.
Time ladies and gentlemen, please,
They both stood up to go,
Walking frames were brought to them,

And heads were bent quite low,
At their homes, both sat in their chairs,
With dreams of days gone by.
Old memories, old dreams, old loves,
Both alone started to cry.

# Ambulance

He sat on the porch, just looking,
Looking at the vehicles go by,
A handkerchief he always carried,
Because he always seemed to have tears in his eyes.
He was looking for a white train
That made a funny noise,
He thought that his wife was in it,
Speeding along so fast.
A bright blue light was on the top,
Was she coming home at last?
He was also very surprised
When the white train passed on by,
It never stopped at his house,
And he didn't hear the reason why.
One night he heard the sound of the white train,
And many people seemed to be in despair,
But he searched and searched for Mabel,
But, of course, she was not there.

## All of Us

How frequently the last time comes, and we do not know,
That this is indeed the last time before all shadows flow,
In the snow of memories locked the gates,
And you only wanted childhood days by a river.

Wandering by the sea, secrets that you've kept,
People that you've met, goodbye is always a warning,
A word we often say when we do not see the morning,
Because death crept in along the way.

# Age

Age is the quality of mind,
If you have left your dreams behind,
If hope is cold, and you no longer look ahead,
If your ambition is totally dead,
Then you are old.

But if from life, you take the best,
If in life, you keep your head up high,
No matter how the years go by,
No matter how the birthplace flies,
Then, my dear, you'll never be old.

# A Women's Refuge

Inside the house filled with noise,
The children play around,
With women's voices loud and clear,
Still, they're afraid, although they're here.
Long narrow halls with pushchairs, boxes full of toys,
Sweets, food and clean clothing for the happy girls and boys.
Various women sit in small groups all around,
Just staring into space, still bearing
The marks of a battered face,
Some of them unkempt, uncared for, exhausted but doing
their best
To have a rest from the beatings, and in return, face
homelessness.
One child curled up in a blanket,
With two black eyes at least, and her matted hair
Was caked in blood, stuck to the side of her face.
Her mother clinging to her baby,
Who constantly would cry,
And when the cover was removed, you could see the reason why.
For the baby was covered in bruises,
Yellow, black and blue,
And its arms, they were just hanging, the way broken arms do.
In the corner, a little boy crying,
Holding onto his mother's skirt with tears in his eyes.
He just looked up and said, "Mummy, please help me; it hurts."

# Wandering Mind

Lying in bed, my mind starts to wander,
To a place where your laughter mingles with mine,
Like bells chiming away in the breeze of summer,
Our bodies so close, our fingers entwined.

A place where our pride fades away in the sunlight,
Defences forgotten and fear disappears,
And when one looks in the eyes of the other,
We know why we waited for all of these years.

Then all the others and all of the heartbreaks,
All the events that led us to now,
They all seemed so distant yet perfectly written,
Since I see that they brought us together somehow.

But the scene shattered, eyes fluttered open,
And all I see is the dark of the night,
And I realise with sadness, as I do so often,
Our story is mine, and mine only to write.

# Can You

Can you spare a moment?
Do you have time to spare?
Can you slow down and talk to me?
Please find time to care.
Can you spare a moment?
Please do the best you can;
I know I'm a drunken fool,
And a very unhappy man.
Please slow down and talk to me,
If only someone would,
But everyone just walks on by,
I may as well be a block of wood.
So, can you spare a moment,
In this world today for me?
I guess you can't, so just go away,
Tomorrow is another day.

# Boxer Bob

He goes with his basket and slow feet,
He sells his fruit from street to street,
His two black eyes are legend from his boxing times,
For this is Boxer Bob.
The man who had muscles harder than
A schoolboy's bones,
Who could hold his ground when six tall boys played around.

Small children, now, they have no grace,
Can steal his fruit before his face,
And when he threatens with his hands,
Mock him two feet from where he stands.
Mock him, who could some years ago,
Have leapt five feet to strike a blow.

Poor Bob, I remember when
You were a god to many men,
But now you pass you on the street,
Not knowing who you are;
You are the man who kept bad people away,
And always would have anyway.

# Courage

As you read this poem,
Perhaps you'd like to know,
That this story really happened many years ago,
When two talented young artists,
Were struggling hard to earn,
Just enough to live on,
So both of them could learn,
How to be great artists,
And leave behind a name,
That many centuries later,
Would still retain its fame.
But in their dire necessity,
For the warmth of food and fire,
One of the last is sacrificed,
His dreams and heart desire,
So he might earn a living and provide enough to eat,
So both of them were back again,
Secure on their two feet.
But months and years of grovelling,
Destroyed the craftsman's touch –
His hands, they couldn't work anymore,
Those hands that promised so much.
He could no longer hold a brush
The way he used to do,
And the dreams he wanted and cherished,
No longer could come true,
With his friend who had succeeded,

Who now could purchase all the things,
That once, they had so badly needed –
What had he done?
He had sacrificed his fame and success,
For another man's dream of happiness.

# Existence

You had an easy existence and a cosy country place,
With hardly a wrinkle at 70 on your face,
Growing old, with books and all the wine,
With a beautiful grace, unaware you have no place,
In this new complicated world of ours.

Incompatibility of taste, uncommon with that of your man,
You have a love of gardening and a very snug estate,
With dogs and your grown-up children,
And, of course, staying in bed, getting up late.

You have no religion or imagination and a hazy view of life,
You never hold your husband, though you were his wife,
He feels sad and lonely and does not understand
Why he loves you so very much and cannot let you go.

His life seems to be in a different world, things crop up now
and then,
He has a life caring for his wife; his friends pop in now and again,
They complain that life is short, not enough time.

They go to the pub, to the club for bingo and social occasions,
but for Albert, life is just too long in a different kind of way,
He wishes she was gone.

# I Wanted

I wanted and wanted so much to be like you,
To laugh and do the things you do,
To understand and be understood,
Wouldn't it be nice if only we could?

But I am old; people do not see,
The other side of what is me,
I am trapped inside my mind,
But maybe I can teach mankind.

A very simple rhyme,
Laughter, patience, strength and trust,
All the things we need to know,
That make us understand how life has to go,
To meet up in His promised land.

# Earthquakes

Panic, fear, the waves follow,
Nothing's clear, no shelter, no clothes,
What happened, no one knows;
Crushed and hurt, fear of death,
And covered in dirt.
You hear the beginnings of cries and pain,
"Help me, I'm here," but all in vain,
No warnings, no signs,
Scared for life, everyone fears.
No clean water,
Just people struggling to live,
So, if we are kind people, please let us give.

# Don't be Cruel

Don't be cruel, don't be mean,
Don't tell lies, don't be obscene,
Don't be belittled, don't be mad,
Be grateful for all you have had.

Do be kind, do be true,
Do listen to each point of view,
Do be honest, also be fair,
Do take time to show you care.

Respect others as you like to be respected,
Make sure each task is completed,
Don't hold grudges or speak revolting words,
And never regret things that you have done.

Tomorrow is a new day,
And your dreams have just not happened yet,
And with this information, life should be on an even keel;
Let's hope your tomorrows, will be better than your yesterdays.

# In My Home

It's good to see familiar things,
The things of everyday,
The useful items and the ones
Just there for display.
The chair that is comfortable,
The chair is fading true,
But that chair could tell you a thing or two.
A useful kitchen stool,
I have had for many a year,
And the cup and saucer that always bring a tear –
They have a special meaning,
No money would it make,
You see that cup and saucer, that's mine.
A vase for pretty flowers, a horseshoe up above,
A picture of our wedding day was given to us with love.
I will not be moving anywhere,
This is my home, you'll see; you'll never catch me.

# I Woke Up

I woke up this morning,
And was feeling rather good,
Wondering why I felt this way,
And if I really should.
It's not because of anything,
Or what I thought of today,
Or anyone that came to visit me that day.
What should I do this morning,
To make my day just right,
Apart from all the unusual jobs,
That come within my site?
I thought of all the wonderful things,
And how the smile on my husband's face makes me glad,
I thought about Pumpkin and Porky
And the other animals we've had.
I thought about Paul's mum and dad,
And all the love and joy we share,
I thought about our own children,
That mostly give us pleasure.
And I thank the Lord for waking me up,
For giving me the chance to remember
My good luck.

# I Wanted

I wanted health and strength to do great things,
I wanted enough patience for each day,
I wanted to be strong, sensitive and true,
I wanted wealth, happiness and ease,
But poverty prevailed; it made me wise.
I wanted power to conquer and to please,
But duty came along and gave me self-discipline,
I wanted a wonderful home,
Filled with love, nothing to be frightened of,
And then you came along, and I felt at ease.
Through the years we've been together,
And we've been through some stormy weather,
We seem to have had a lot of disasters,
The kind you cannot make better with a plaster;
We got through, me and you.

# I Remember

I remember him holding my hand,
I remember him looking at me,
I remember him giving me promises,
For a lifetime, I remember him.

I remember him walking with me,
Us holding each other's hands,
I remember him carrying me shoulder-high,
Because I told him my legs hurt;
He knew the reason why.

It was time for her to go to bed
So, on shoulders high, she was taken home.
Many stories were read as she was put to bed –
That was my dad.

# His Mind

His mind tends to backtrack
He can scale the Pyrenees
In his mind, he can run a marathon
And climb the biggest trees
In his mind, he built lots of extensions
And put the world to rights
And all before breakfast
Or rather sleepless nights
His mind is strong and active
There's nothing he can't do
His mind is only 26, but in real life, he's 72.

# Happy Place

It used to be a happy room,
Full of joy and sun; now it's an empty room,
No sign of anyone.
No money in the meter,
No food inside the fridge,
Just damp and emptiness.
There's dust along the window ledge,
There's dust upon the floor,
A piano in the corner
Not played anymore.
But it is this empty room
Where four small children used to play,
And sing songs around the table next to a Christmas tree.
But what is the point of a great big house
When you live alone,
Where memories are safe inside?
Oh, I must stop all this pity and my pride.
The car is coming to pick me up,
In the nursing home is where I'll finish my life.

# Happy Days

These days there is not so much spring in my step,
Gone are the days when I could spin and dance,
Yet, deep down inside, I'm exactly the same,
From a Miss to a Mrs, a girl to a wife,
I love my family as much as I can.

The wrinkles have multiplied the same as the years,
Where did they go, my hopes, dreams and fears?
I walk slowly, my hair a little grey; did it happen yesterday?

But I still love every moment of my life,
My heart still wants to sing, and I shiver with delight,
For I am happy and loved, the pathway is bright,
I may need glasses, my hearing is not keen,
But I know where I'm going, and I know where I've been.

# The Gossip

Although she is not old or young,
This woman with the serpent tongue,
The knowing look, the beady eyes,
She twists the words to tell,
Some gossip.

But this woman with the serpent tongue,
Did evil words, not filled with bliss,
Her poisoned tongue can hardly wait,
Exchanging details to relate.

Did you know, his wife and lover
Has left her husband for another,
She's taken the car and left him at home,
To care for three children all on his own.

The truth is that young Maggie Brown,
Had to leave that busy town,
To be beside her dying brother,
And to ease the pain of her sick mother.

So, if the gossip comes to tell you,
The things other people say and do,
Pity her, for maybe her own life,
Is full of bitterness and strife.

# Life Goes Running

Life goes by, and it will leave,
Good days, bad days,
Storms and calm,
Born stars in the sky,
Comets are formed in the universe,
Rivers flow into the sea,
The waves in the pack,
And the smell of the sea,
Fill us with melancholy.
The trees are dressed green,
Spring flowers in bright colours,
That fill us with joy,
And make our days happy.
But then three comes,
Sadness softly,
Because our beautiful dream ended,
The night ended,
And a day will start,
And everything returns to its place.
This is all part of nature,
And the life of any person
That inhabits this planet,
Which is called Earth.

# Let It Be Me

Apply to win the lottery, let it be me,
I won't be mean, I will give some to charity,
Then I could leave this world of stress behind,
Could you send the money by express!
Go on, let it be me.

Come on, come on, Camelot,
There are things about my life you just can't know,
We are poor beyond compare,
And my cupboards are almost bare,
So, you see,
Some money would be good for me.

I know some poor people,
Their lives are filled with care,
I understand that some live in cardboard boxes,
I wish I could give them a mansion, food and drink,
I wouldn't mind if they won the lottery,
But let it be me.

We wouldn't have to stay indoors,
The post would be fine,
We wouldn't bother about interest rates,
And we would want to go to France or Rome,
We would both rather stay at home.

# Simon

Little Simon, he went playing in the park not far from home,
His brother, he went with him so he wouldn't be alone,
A stranger went up to Simon, he just ran away,
He didn't eat the ice cream that was given him that day.
A moment later, his brother looked around,
He saw a shoe of Simon's lying on the ground,
He heard his brother screaming and saw him dragged away,
Both boys had been traumatised from that very day.

# Teacher or Undertaker

Failure should be our teacher, not our undertaker –
Failure is a delay, not defeat,
It is a temporary detour, not a dead end,
Failure is something we can avoid only by saying nothing,
Doing nothing and being nothing.

Learn from the past, set vivid, detailed goals
For the future, and live in only a moment of time,
Over which you have control now!

People spend a lifetime searching for happiness,
Looking for peace,
They chase ideal dreams, addictions, religions,
Even other people, hoping to fill the emptiness that plagues them.
The irony is that the only place they ever need to
Search is within themselves.

When you have a positive frame of mind,
You broadcast positive thoughts and feelings,
To the world around you.

It is faith in something and enthusiasm in something,
That makes life worth living.

Obstacles don't have to stop you,
If you run into a wall, don't turn around
And give up,
Figure out how to climb it, go through it,
Or work around it.

# Sod's Law

If you stay in for a package,
To be delivered to your door,
Something really important,
That you've been waiting for,
You stay within the sounds of your doorbell,
You've been in all morning, and there have been no sounds,
And you just pop out and put the washing on the line,
And sure he won't come if you run,
Back indoors, there's a card on the mat,
I tried to deliver your parcel today,
And I cannot record it,
So I drove away.

# Poppies

Poppies blooming, growing red,
On the Flanders fields are spread,
Covering our fallen dead in a distant land.
Poppies growing in the lane,
Bringing their memories back again,
Through the mist of time and plain,
To their native land.
Poppies woven in a wreath,
Poppies wet with tears and grief,
While last memory to bequeath,
To their roll of honour.
Let us never ever forget,
Let us remember the enormous debt
We owe to these brave men,
Who met death in a foreign land.

# Old

What's the date? What's the time?
She's got to get it right,
For in her diary she wrote:
"It's the worst day of my life,
They're coming to take me away, you see,
Put me in an old folk's home,
So what is the date? What is the time?
I've got to get it right,
All my treasures are around me,
Treasures that are mine,
I can take a few pieces,
But I am crying for the things that I have left behind."

# Wonderful Land

There's a wonderful land where I go by myself,
Without getting out of chair,
I just take a book from the library shelf,
Turn its pages, and pretend I am there.
In that wonderful country of yesterday,
Where tomorrows always knew,
But the African sands burn in the African sun.
Where the north shivers under the snow,
Over the mountains and valleys
Where strange rivers blow.
I share in the magic of fairies and gnomes,
I have read all about mermaids under the sea,
I have studied the fish and their watery homes
And the birds and the ants and the bees.
But I am old now, I cannot see these things,
That's why I live in a wonderful land by myself,
Without getting out of my chair,
For my memories will always be there.

# Where Do the Birds Go?

Where do the birds go in their endless flight?
When the guns of war fired,
And the birds go off in fright,
And we do not miss them going,
And we do not miss their song,
For our ears are listening,
To the battle song.
We stand on the British earth beneath
British sky,
And the birds,
I believe, flock southward,
Wheeling as they fly.
And there is a morning mist,
And the trees turn brown,
And the wind blows and blows,
All the dead leaves down,
And lamps are early lit,
And curtains early drawn,
And nights have frozen dewdrops,
That are on the ground.
And just the same as the German earth,
And just the same as the German sky,
I don't know why we had a war,
So many people had to die.

# Think

The tapping gets louder,
I stop and look behind,
The man approaches,
I could that see he was blind.
We wait together at the crossing,
Standing shoulder to shoulder,
The cars and lorries roll on by,
But there isn't anyone to bother.
The signal changes, and he starts to cross,
Tapping away across a busy street,
I stand and watch him on his way,
I wonder how he copes each day.
For him, darkness has no colour,
Nor flowers, sunset or blue skies,
Now when you're feeling down,
And your spirits were high,
Just think of this world,
And close your eyes.

# There Is Nothing

There is nothing that makes you frustrated,
Any frustration you experience is the result of,
Your own choice to react with frustration.

There is nothing that makes you annoyed,
Any annoyance you experience comes about because,
You have decided to be annoyed.

You can choose to be annoyed,
Frustrated,
Angry,
And spiteful,
But you can also choose not to be.

Imagine how effective you could be,
If there was nothing that annoyed you;
That level of effectiveness is yours to choose,
Right here, right now.

All sorts of things will happen in your world today,
You can let them get to you, annoy and frustrate you,
Or you can choose to follow your own path.

You have the power to be free of frustration,
Free of annoyance,
Free to accomplish and enjoy life,
Choose that freedom today.

# *Family*

# Our Family Album

We have a family album, it's like a family tree,
I slowly turn the pages and the pictures I can see,
It starts off with grands and greats,
Then slowly down the line,
Like a book of history, a journey going on through time.
Fashions start to alter, beards they come and go,
Ladies' skirts go up and down, a proper fashion show,
Pictures turned to colour,
Black and white have gone,
A different place, a different time, so much to look upon.
But what is so amazing,
Is the likeness we can see,
Showing up in the genes,
Right through our family tree.

# A Poem for My Mother

I miss you so much,
Your laugh, your smile, your touch,
You always brightened my days,
With all the smiles you sent my way.
I need you as my angel,
To always be at my side,
I need you as my angel
To give me peace of mind.
I like to think you're near to me, to know that you are there,
Even though I can't see you,
I feel that you are near.
Please do not forget me, Mum,
For you are always in my heart, my thoughts, and prayers.

I love you.

# A Mother's Crown

Heaven lit up with His mighty presence,
As all the angels looked down,
Today the Lord was placing jewels,
In all the mothers' crowns.

As He held up a golden crown,
As all the mothers looked on,
He said in His gentle voice,
"I just want to explain each stone."

He held the first gem in His hand,
But the radiance couldn't match his own,
For He was the light of heaven,
Reflecting off each of the stones.

The first gem, He said, is an emerald
And it's for endurance alone,
For all the nights you waited up for your children to come home,
For all the nights by their bedside,
You stayed till the fever went down,
For nursing every little wound,
I add this emerald to your crown.

A ruby I'll place by the emerald,
For leading your child in the right way,
For if you hadn't taught them all about me,
They wouldn't be here with you today.
For always being right there,
Through all life's important events,
I give you a sapphire stone for the time and love you spent.

# Hard for a Boy

Mothers, it's hard for boys to say I Love You,
It's very hard to show how much we care,
It's hard to put arms around you,
And say thank you for always being there.
Thanks for wiping away the tears,
Thanks for taking away all my fears,
Thanks for holding me so tight,
When sometimes, I used to cry at night.
When I came in with muddy knees,
And the cuts upon my face,
You never ever told me off,
You grinned, and I felt at ease,
Because you knew I'd never be bad,
Because you brought me up
In that kind of way,
I am so proud to be your son,
And give this card to you on Mother's Day.

# Grandmothers

God, in His loving and all-wise ways,
Made your heart that once was young and sweet,
Serene and more gentle and less restless too,
Content to remember the joys it once knew,
And all that is on the pathway to pleasure,
Is but a memory to cherish and to treasure.
And so your springtime will be sweet to recall,
The autumn of life is the best time of all,
For the childlike wildness of our youth
Has gradually ceased,
Leaving us memories and peace.

# Mother's Love

Sometimes we feel the things we do,
Could never be enough for you,
We give our all, we always will,
You think for us life has stood still.
The years go by in such a flurry, to you all we do is worry;
It's only because we love and care,
And let you know we are always there.
For years the harvest time decays too much,
Seems like a crime,
But you will look back one day and see,
I don't want you to be like me, I want you to be free.
The world has changed, that's why we worry,
And you want to grow up in a hurry,
The time will come when you will know,
That I taught you all you needed to know.

# In the Dark Womb

In the dark womb where I began,
My mother's life made me woman,
Through all the myth of human birth,
Her beauty fed my common earth.
I cannot see, nor breathe, nor stir,
But through the death of some of her,
Down in the darkness of the grave,
She cannot see the life she gave.
For all her love, she cannot tell,
Whether I used it ill or well.
If the grave's gate could be undone,
She would know what I had begun;
I am grown and wish she could see,
What has become of me.

# My Home

You know, it's good to see familiar things,
The things that you see every single day,
The useful items and the ones that are purposely out,
For display.
A chair that is comfortable,
But very old,
A small table and a footstool,
Some colours that seemed so bright,
A useful kitchen tool.
A vase to hold fresh cut flowers,
A pretty china plate,
One that has no special name,
Nor money would never make.
The comfort of a well-known thing,
Like the things my husband used to make,
I have a fine-looking ottoman,
A bureau,
The best ever seen,
Tables, chairs and benches,
Wonderful things that you wouldn't believe.
He's a craftsman with a wonderful gift,
That makes me very proud,
To be the wife of such a wonderful man,
I am so proud of all the things my wonderful husband has done.

# My Dog

I left her lying peacefully,
On the table at the vet's,
I had to have her put to sleep,
Like some of my other pets.
She gave me so much pleasure,
In the years that we had together,
With the angels and her dad,
So, I left her lying peacefully,
On the vet's table.
Knowing where she was going,
It wasn't to be that bad,
But when I went indoors
And sat on my chair and looked around,
My dog wasn't there.
My heart is truly broken,
And my love for her will stay,
Other people thought of her as a dog,
But for me, my child and company.

# My Dad

I remember him holding my hand,
I remember him looking after me,
I remember him giving promises for a lifetime,
I just remember him being my dad.
I remember him walking with me, hand in hand,
Telling me things I don't understand.
I remember being on his shoulders very high,
"Carry me home; my legs ache",
And I began to cry.
"Dad, my legs are hungry," and he would reply,
"And so am I,"
Put me down on the floor,
I cannot go any faster,
"Have a rest then,"
We will not have any disasters.

# Mother, Mothers

Mother and son,
I say, soldier, tell us the tricks of the trade,
The passing of your hours,
Tell me all the plans that you have made.
What you think about transformation,
From boyhood to a man,
What's it like to be a soldier?
Now you can.
And what can I say?
What is my reply?
There is no answer,
But I see the fear in your eyes,
For when you marched away that day,
With your rifle and your pack,
I must have somehow misunderstood,
I thought my son would be coming back.
So, what could I say?
What could I do?
There's no answer,
But I see the fear in your young eyes,
So, you see my dear,
It wasn't fair.
When he walked away that day,
A young boy just 17 years old,
You were still old enough to stay,
But for your country you thought it wise,
To help as much as you could,
But, my dear, you should come back,
The whole war was just misunderstood.

# My Sister

What has happened to my sister?
Oh, goodness me, where can she be?
She didn't sleep in her room last night,
That's unusual, you see.
Why is her window open, Mum?
The curtains blowing free,
And there is a circle of dust,
Where her money box used to be.
Why do you turn your head away, ma'am,
And why do the teardrops fall?
Why did you crumple that note in your hand?
And you say it was nothing at all.

During the night I heard someone crying, Mum,
Crying in anger or in pain,
And now, please tell me, Mum,
Why did she run off in the rain?
Why are your eyes red, Mum?
And why haven't you combed your hair?
And why are you sitting, all of the time,
Right next to the telephone?
What's happened to my sister, Mum?
What has happened to her?
I love her, you see, she is so close to me,
And I can't see her anywhere.

# Teenager

Teenager life; what a bore,
Go to your room,
Don't slam the door,
"No way,"
In a minute, maybe later,
To understand parents, you need a translator.
Why is it that,
When you answer back,
Our parents say "Do you want a smack?"
"Get out of this room,"
I hold up a fist,
"How do I know? And I'll never be missed."
What an embarrassment,
Life can be,
When you're a teenager,
Just like me.

# Stepmother's Day

Each year I look, but I can't see,
A card that tells the truth,
A card that cancels out a hurt,
The bitterness and the ghost.
I read these lines and secretly,
Just turn away,
For as a child I did not give,
Cards on Mother's Day.
Now I have learnt to love you,
And I'm contented in every way,
So now I know I can gladly send,
This card on Mother's Day.

Thinking I had been such a fool,
There is something that I need to know,
Was it because of me, you had to go?
Or was it that someone else loved you?
Were you, like me, crying at night?
Did you get so scared that you wet the bed?
Did you ever wish that you were dead?
I did, Mother.
Now that you're old, sick and lonely,
Your thoughts turn back to me,
Your lover is dead, so is my dad,
That all seems very sad.
Now, what shall I do?
Do I turn my back on you?
Well, Mother, it just has to be,
The future isn't ours, you see.

# You Got It from Your Father

It was the best he had to give,
And gladly he bestowed it, it's yours while you live,
You may claim the watch he gave you, and another you may
claim it,
It was a fine day when you got it, and a worthy name to wear,
When he took it from his father, there was no dishonour there,
Through the years he proudly wore it,
And to his father he was true,
And your name was clear and spotless when he passed it on to you.
Oh, there's much that he has given and that he values not at all,
And has watched you break your playthings,
In the days when you were small,
And you've lost the knife he gave, and you scattered many
a game,
But you'll never hurt your father if you're careful with his name.
It is yours to wear forever,
Yours to wear while you live,
And when a child is born,
It is yours to give.

# What Riches Have You

What riches have you,
That you deem me poor?
I have twenty-four hours each day;
Do you have more?

I have never gone hungry,
These things I perceive as wealth:
The comfort of my home,
A sound mind, a body in good health.

I love the beauty of this place,
The mountains, never twice the same,
I live the rhythms of the season,
Can you make the same claim?

People, friends, family – precious treasures all –
My children and grandchildren, too,
We laugh and talk and give of self,
O, I have riches, indeed I do!

# To A Daughter

I know right now it's hard to put your finger,
On the things that hurt the most,
Especially when you're mixed and can't tell angel from ghost,
Because here in the real world,
It just isn't easy at all,
When someone hurts you,
Goodness me, it's real tears that fall.
A heart can soon get broken, it's said,
But you wouldn't listen to me,
Whatever advice I gave you,
It only made you mad.
Instead of giving you advice,
I should have been quiet,
And let you deal with the problems you have.
So, if you need teardrops,
As they have so often fallen,
Think about other people,
The way they think of you,
Then you will be,
My loving daughter,
And together, we will see it through.

# The Waiting Room

We wait our turn as still as mice,
For medicine and free advice,
Two mothers with their little girls,
One with straight hair, one with curls,
And I myself the last to come,
Looked around at everyone;
Some shabbily dressed I could see,
And I wondered what they thought of me.
One woman dressed in finest clothes,
Started to look down her nose,
The other mother poorly dressed,
Holding a baby to her breast,
The other woman gave a wicked stare,
And the other two children, sitting there,
Took advantage of that site,
They made faces full of spite.
But this poor woman said not a word,
But from the other woman's lips I heard,
"Why has this come to be?
Me in such ragged company,"
The ragged woman's looks replied,
"If you can dress with so much pride,
Why are you here so neat and nice,
For medicine free and free advice?"

# The Idiot

The idiot, she lived in the house where she was born,
No wonder she looks so tired and worn,
With her, lived her son,
Fifty years,
The son had caused her many tears,
For he had been an idiot all of his life,
Since she'd given birth to him when a very young wife.
When others laughed then he would weep,
And never find the need to sleep,
Her other son, new to married life,
Lived with the pair, and his young wife,
They had a baby, just three months old,
This son, his brother, would often scold,
For although he loved the baby boy,
He treated him as a toy,
And with his rough hands he used to play,
And mark the child mostly every day,
This scene was the recipe for domestic strife,
It was the mother, the idiot and his brother's wife.
The husband came home and each night regaled,
He was fed up with domestic strife,
When the elderly mother was out one day,
The idiot picked up the child to play,
He started to throw the child up in the air,
And laughed at the child's screams without a care,
Some people in white came to take him away,
And over and over these words he would say,
"Idiot loves you, idiot cares, idiot loves you,

73

And nobody's there."
The idiot picked up the child to play,
He started to throw the child up in the air,
And laughed at the child's screams, without a care,
Some people in white came to taking him away,
And over and over these words he would say,
"Idiot loves you, idiot cares, idiot loves you,
And nobody's there."

# The Cat

You seem amused that I just sat,
And wrapped a present for my cat,
Complete with paper tag and bow,
Then hidden it so he wouldn't know,
Till Christmas day; what is there inside?
In fact, you laughed and also cried,
You also giggled secretly,
If you saw the gift the cat gave me.
We're friends, you see, he and I,
That's why he gets cross when I cry,
I patch him up when he's been in a fight,
And he keeps my feet warm at night.
Now, all of this means it's time for our lunch,
You out there wouldn't enjoy what we will have,
We start with tuna chunks in brine,
The cat's is plain, I have sauce on mine,
The turkey, we both like the breast,
I always have to think what to do with the rest,
I will think about that another day,
For it's Christmas now,
And I'll be going out to play.

# Religion

# A Christmas Card

The gentle little Jesus child,
Came as a gift of love,
From his father up in heaven,
With a message from above.
His birth was in a stable
In Bethlehem, we know,
And the miracle happened centuries ago.
So little baby Jesus,
Came down on Earth did well,
And lived among his people,
And looked after them as well.

# Blessed

Blessed are they that understand my faults, yet still they call,
Blessed are they that strain to hear what people say.
Blessed are they that seem to know,
That my eyes are dim, my wits are slow.
Blessed are they who looked away,
When I spilled coffee on the table the other day.

Blessed are they with a cheery smile,
Who stopped to talk to me for a while,
Blessed are they that never say,
"You've told me the same story twice today".

Blessed are they who know the way to try and bring,
Back stories of yesterday,
Blessed are they who make it known,
That I'm loved and respected and not alone.

For although I am tired, bent and old,
And there are lots of things that I cannot remember,
I would hate to live in this room alone, be it
Springtime, or even December.

# God Has a Plan

God has a plan for each of us,
I have a feeling that there is
A wonderful plan for you,
I pray that the paths you walk,
And the roads you travel will take
You to amazing places –
Places where you see the possibilities,
Where you discover what it is like
When dreams come true,
And the promise,
The potential of all the wonderful
Qualities that are inside you,
But you are not born yet.
I pray that God's plan will
Bring out the best in you,
I pray that people in your life,
Appreciate what is so
Special about a new baby,
A new life, a new bringing,
You do not know us yet,
But one day you will.
Be proud of your mum and dad,
Because they are so proud of you.

# Jim

Chemotherapy was the game she played with her teddy bear,
She had a teddy bear hospital, and each teddy had no hair.
She had a special teddy bear,
Its name was simply Jim,
She talked to Jim when she was lonely or depressed,
She told Jim everything because he knew it was for the best.
Jim, you see, got better,
He wasn't hairless like the rest,
It was on a cold December night when God took her away,
To where
There is no pain, only happiness and play.
And in her tiny coffin, lined up on every side,
Were all the other teddy bears with eyes still open wide.
The teddies, they all had shaved heads,
And were dressed in clothes of white,
She knew that she was dying,
And had dressed them during the night.
She had spoken to Jim about it, and they thought it was for
the best,
For all the other teddy bears were tired and needed a rest.
Round the tree were flowers,
Roses were planted there,
And sitting proudly at the top was Jim,
And I know this seems silly that when people pass that way,
Jim seems, to them, to be crying, because he's a lonely bear today.

# The Loom of Time

Man's life is laid in the loom of time,
To a pattern he doesn't see,
While the weavers work and the shuttles fly,
To the dawn of eternity.

Some shuttles are filled with silver threads,
And some with treats of gold,
While often the darker colours,
Are all that they may hold.

The weaver works with skilful eye,
Each shuttle flies to and from,
He sees the pattern so clear,
In case it could go wrong.

God surely planned the pattern,
Each thread, the dark and the fair,
He's chosen his master skill
And place in the web with care.

He only knows its beauty,
Because of how it was made,
The dark threads were needed in the weaver's hand,
And the threads of gold and silver
Were the things
That we needed to understand.

# Peace of Mind

This is the most powerful aid to peace of mind,
We often develop ill feelings inside of our heat,
For the person who insults us or harms us.

We nurture grievances,
Which in turn results in loss of sleep,
Development of stomach ulcers,
And high blood pressure.

This insult or injury was done once,
But nourishing of grievance goes on forever,
By constantly remembering it.

Get over this bad habit,
Believe in the justice of God,
Let Him judge the act of the one who insulted you,
Life is too short to waste in such trifles.
Forgive,
Forget,
And march on;
Love flourishes in giving and forgiving.

# The Wind at the Window

It's almost dawn, and I'm warm between the sheets and blankets,
Dream it all or nothing,
Behold, suddenly something wakes me up –
It is the home of the window that stirs,
Looking like someone wants to enter,
And I look around me, scared to understand that there is no,
It is only the wind that in all its fury shakes.
Look through the window,
And my God! What a sight,
The strength of the nature,
Showing its power,
The tumble-down trees almost,
The leaves are carried by the wind in an endless swirl,
But the tree outside my window,
In its majestic pose,
Resisting, remains standing.
But depending on the gusts bending, who insist on shaking,
To see that scene makes me cold,
I return to my warm bed to try and sleep,
Thinking, perhaps, that not far away,
Someone is facing the storm.
I am so thankful to my gracious God,
To have a roof and a warm bed,
Where I can hold,
I lie awake listening to the wind!
Whistling, howling,
Seems that it sings a song,
I cannot understand,
Just know that it is the nature, showing all his power.

# The Praying Hands

The praying hands are much, much more,
Than just works of art;
They are the souls of creation,
Of a deeply thankful heart.
They are a masterpiece,
That love alone could paint,
And they reveal the selfishness
Of an unheard saint.
These hands so scarred and worn,
Tell the story of a man,
Who sacrificed his talent
In accordance with God's plan,
For in God's plan are many things,
Meeting cannot understand,
But we must trust God's judgement,
And be guided by his hand.
Sometimes he asks us to give up
Dreams of happiness,
Sometimes we must forget our hopes,
Of fortune and success.
Not all of us can triumph,
Or rise to heights of fame,
And many times that would be ours,
Goes to another man's name.
But he who makes a sacrifice,
So another may succeed,
Is indeed a true disciple,

Of our blessed Saviour's creed.
For when we give ourselves away,
To sacrifice and love,
We are laying out riches,
For ourselves up above.

# *Love*

# Just Absence

Eyes are closed as I lay,
Yet fear envelopes my aching chest,
And I worry that I will never rest,
Curled up beside you.
So I lay awake and count
The breaths I take,
Each one feeling wasted,
The only piece of you,
Lingers in your absence.

# Lost Love

I think one of the saddest things is,
When two people really get to know
Each other, their secrets, their fears,
Their favourite things, what they love,
Or what they hate, literally everything,
And then they go back to being strangers again.
It's like you have to walk past them,
And pretend like you never knew them,
Yet you know everything about them,
Lost love; where has it gone?

# A Cloud

If only I could die and become a cloud,
And be able to drift across your windowsill,
Would you ever notice me as a cloud,
As I just float in the year?

If love survives earthly death,
And the choice was given to me,
Of course, some days
I would block out the sun,
And make it a miserable day.

Some days you may feel very sad,
And you may have a cloudless sky,
But with love and hope, I'll be there,
I would never leave you alone.

Clouds seem to drift so aimlessly,
Across the summer skies,
Perhaps most of them are lonely souls,
Seeking someone else's eye.

But not mine.
My cloud will be as soft as an angel,
With wings, fluffy and white,
Waiting for you to join me,
Then my wandering would be at an end
Because I can't be half an angel,
When I've lost my husband and my friend.

# Bedtime

Upstairs, the satin sheets await us,
Dark, cold and in anticipation,
Candlelight, flame blazing slow,
We slide into bed, pulses racing,
Bodies warm, soon in a tangle,
Loving thoughts in our minds,
Touching, kissing, stroking hair,
Soft breathing fills the air.
We cuddle up in the candle's glow,
The candle now burnt down quite low,
The love we found so long ago,
Is just as wonderful tonight,
As it was in the beginning.

# Another Chance

How often we wish for another chance,
To make a fresh beginning,
A chance to block out our mistakes,
Change failure into winning.

And it does not take a special time,
To make a brand-new start,
It only takes the deep desire,
To try with all our heart,
To live a little better, always be forgiving,
To add a little sunshine,
To the world in which we're living.

So never give up in despair,
And think that you are through,
For there's always a tomorrow,
And a chance to start anew.

# Darling

To hear your gentle breathing,
As you lay by my side,
To wake up to your perfect
Face and smile,
Makes life worthwhile.
To say your name,
To kiss your cheek,
To hold you in my arms,
To lay my head upon your chest,
These are the things
I love the best –
Nothing else matters.

# Close Together, Far Apart

We live close together and so far apart,
Joy in our faces and grief in our heart,
There is no common ground left between us at all,
But we love our children, so helpless and small.

Who would have foreseen it would turn out this way?
No lover, no friend at the end of the day.

Must we be joined in a battle of wills, who pays the mortgage?
And which one of the bills?
Who gets custody, who will it be? or
Who gets the holidays – you or me?
When can they come, and how soon must they leave?
Who gets the birthdays?
Who gets Christmas Eve?

Who runs to comfort the cry in the dark?
Who gets weekends and a walk in the park?
It's business as usual; divorce is no shame,
Oh, where will I be?
When I'm calling their names.

# Life

Life; is it fair?
And of happiness; is your full share ready?
Have you sometimes
Felt really down,
Sometimes for which,
You are not renowned?
And the reasons,
You don't really know why;
Is it because someone's
Hurt you and made you cry?
Well, these things happen
Now and again,
And sometimes remedies can
Drive you insane,
Because you feel lost
And confused, and inside your heart feels bruised,
It is aching and full of hurt,
Because someone has thrown
Some dirt in your face;
There is no simple answer
To these problems because emotions are often complicated.
Throwaway shadow across the light,
And you cannot see right from wrong,
How difficult that is to do,
To discard your feelings, it's not easy for you,
Because the feelings in your heart are part of you,
And the emotions are easy to act,

Face the cold and maybe cruel fact,
Because they will protect you and hide the truth
Away in the dark,
Never daring to cling to the truth,
That someone hurt your heart.

# Look At Her

Look at her powdered white face,
I wonder when she last saw the sun,
Look at her worn-out shoes and clothes,
I wonder where she came from.

Look at her sitting on the swing,
Holding the chain of the swing in each hand,
Trying to remember
What her legs should do,
Shall I go over and help?

Some giggling children run forward,
By this time she had started to swing,
The tears in her eyes were marvellous,
Then suddenly she started to sing.

She laughed, and she played with the children,
On a level no others could see,
At the end of the day, she said, "Listen,
Come closer and stand near me.

"I have blue spotted bread in my bread bin,
I wear jumpers three at a time,
My kettle,
Well, I don't have one,
Silly me, I just burnt it dry.

"I have had a fun day,
With all you children,"
And then she gave a heavy sigh.

She waved to the children,
As she walked off in the distance,
Leaving the children with tears in their eyes.

# Mr. Grey

It was a tiny, quiet room,
Not a sound could I hear,
Then I turned around to look at you,
And there was nobody there,
So, I got up to go outside,
And to my great surprise,
You stood on the doorstep,
With teardrops in your eyes.
You look across to where I stood,
And raised your hat to me,
You really knew not who I was,
That was plain to see,
I lead you by the hand indoors,
I try to make you understand,
That other clothing should be worn,
On such a distinguished man.
By the time we'd finished speaking,
And wiped away each other's tears,
And I told you that we were married,
And we had been for many years,
You walked with me into a room,
Naked, you lay on the bed,
And I covered you up with a blanket,
And these are the words that I said;
"I'm sorry if I hurt you,
And if I made you cry,
I do many strange things,
Darling, I don't know the reason why,

I just forget that you're my wife and I want to run away,
But then you always get me back,
And make me want to stay."
I stroked his hair like always,
And I held him close to me,
I hummed his favourite tunes,
And then he hummed them back to me,
That was the way our life had to be.

# Love Is Like Candlelight

Love is like candlelight,
Glowing in the dark,
The warmness kindles,
From a tiny spark.

The light is soft at first,
Then, it grows bright,
For some, it grows over time,
For some, it's love at first sight.

If not taken care of,
The flame will slowly die,
And when it's gone, it leaves you,
Sitting there, wondering why.

# Old Love

How many times have people lain beneath the tree,
That will not seek shade again;
How many lovers kissed and ran,
To melt like snowflakes in the sun,
Their lips cold now, no passion craved,
But lie forgotten in the grave?

How many through the woods to walk?
Together side by side,
Their hands entwined like painted flowers,
That blossom in the summer shows
How often they wished time would stand still,
And now they sleep,
They surely will.

# No One Can Speak of True Love

No one can speak of true love,
If you have no idea what it is to share
Life with someone for so long.
True love, real love,
Is far beyond romanticism,
And does not have much to do with eroticism,
But is linked to work and care,
The two people professed,
Truly committed.

True love
Reveals itself in small gestures,
Day to day and every day.
True love is not selfish,
Is not conceited,
Nor feeds the desire to possess,
The loved one.

Who walks alone,
May even get faster, but he that is accompanied,
Certainly will go farther.

# The Wedding Ring

When my old wedding ring was new,
And each dream that I dreamt could come true,
I remember with pride the day you were my bride,
What a beautiful picture you made by my side.
Even though silver crowns your hair,
I can still see the golden ring that's there,
Love's old flames, it's still the same,
Since the day I changed your name,
When your old wedding ring was new.

# On a First Year of Marriage

It's nice to know two people,
Who love each other the way we do,
Who still find time to hold hands,
And love each other too.
When other people see you,
Give each other an unexpected kiss,
It shows us all that happiness,
Should be like this.

# What Is Love?

What is love?
And why does love never seem to find me?
Instead, broken hearts surround me,
And once again, the wrong man found me,
Saying he wouldn't hurt me,
But in the end, he didn't deserve me.

What is love?
And why doesn't love know my name?
I prayed to God that it would change,
But true love never came.

What is love?
I ask myself time after time;
Why is love so blind,
Or should I not waste my time?
I guess broken hearts are only made for me,
Because love finds everyone else,
But love never found me.

# Time Does Not Bring Relief

Time does not bring relief; you all have lied,
Who told me time would ease me of my pain,
I missed him in the weeping rain,
I want him at high tide,
The old snow melted from mountain side,
And last year's leaves outside his door.
I wish I was beside his side,
But last year's bitter loving must remain,
Heaped on my heart and my old thoughts abide.
There are a hundred places that I fear,
To go with my memory, stays on fire,
And I, into this with grief and relief,
To be in some private plan where I can grieve,
Where never again will I hear defeat.
I will never hear the footsteps or see the face,
I say there is no tomorrow,
All we have is here today.

# The Power of a Hug

There's something in a simple hug,
That always warms the heart,
It welcomes us back home,
And makes it easier to part.
A hug's the way to share the joy,
And sad times we go through,
Or just a way for friends to say,
They like you because you're you.
Hugs are meant for anyone,
For whom we really care,
From your grandma to your neighbour,
Or a cuddly teddy bear.
A hug is an amazing thing,
It's just the perfect way,
To show the love we're feeling,
But can't find the words to say.
It's funny how a little song,
Makes everyone feel good,
In every place and language,
It's always understood.
And hugs don't need equipment,
Special batteries or parts,
Just open up your arms,
And open up your hearts.

# The Village

I wandered through the village, Tom,
And sat beneath the tree,
Beside the recreation ground,
Where we once played, you and me.
But none were there to greet me, Tom,
And few are left to know,
Who played with us upon the grass
Over 50 years ago.
The grass is just the same, Tom,
And children still at play,
The river is still flowing with the Willows by its side,
The Willows are much taller now,
And the river is not so wide.
I saw my first sweetheart, Tom,
As I walked up Parsons Green,
And the memory of my childhood came flooding back again,
She is older now, and I am, Tom,
And perhaps she feels the same,
But I wonder if she, too, wishes for all the old times back again.
I must sound a silly old fool, Tom,
But the tears come to my eyes,
When I thought of her, I loved her so well,
And those early broken ties.
The cemetery was the last call, Tom,
And I took some flowers to lie,
Upon the graves of those I loved,
In far off yesterdays.

# Friendship Is a Ship

Friendship is a ship,
Floating on an ocean of love,
It's that innocent bond,
Like that of the sky's dove.

A true friend in friendship,
Is like a shining jewel,
Which we can't find in heaven,
Neither in hell.

Friendship is an art,
Done from the bottom of the heart,
To be with a friend in gladness,
And support him in sadness.

To be happy and sad in friendship,
Is like sunrise and sunset,
Seeing a friend in tough stages,
One's eyes become wet.

I dream of a friend,
Who will be that good,
Always talking of laughter,
Never being rude.

# Friends or Lovers

Friends or lovers, what shall we be?
Into the future, I cannot see,
But I am sure that of one we will be,
Because you are, for certain, the key.
The future is full of unknown things,
We never know what it will bestow,
Our friendship is one of those things,
Never knowing how far it will go.
You are always in my daily thoughts,
In the coming weeks and months,
What will the future hold for you and me?
The uncertainty, the development,
Will be very exciting for us to see.

# Friends are Eternal

Caring, Sharing, Lending a hand,
Lovers can be forever,
Trusting, giving, thinking of each other,
Friends give hugs,
And comfort in times of need.
Lovers are affectionate and devoted,
Friends – there are many,
Lovers – there should be two,
True friends are forever,
True Lovers are for eternity.
Friend or Lover,
Sometimes it is hard,
To tell the two apart.

# Challenge

Life is a challenge, it is said,
Life is a challenge to all;
A challenge that faces everyone
Whether we rise or we fall.
What is my challenge, I ask?
Now that my sickness has come,
Others are coping, caring has a new era begun.
I no longer will be able to fight,
To reach for a goal to achieve,
No more do I feel that sense of commitment,
Through which my life used to weave.
My body is frail, I know,
But still, I must have something to do,
I should use every muscle, fibre and tissue,
On each of the days that I live.
For today is the challenge,
To battle my way through each day,
Demanding that each day is a tomorrow.

# Sometimes in Life

Sometimes in life you find a special friend,
Someone who changes your life just by being part of it,
Someone who makes you laugh until you can't stop,
Someone who makes you believe that there really is good in
the world,
Someone who convinces you that there really is an unlocked
door just waiting,
For you to open it,
This is forever friendship.

When you're down, and the world seems dark and empty,
Your forever friend lifts you up in spirit,
Makes that dark and empty world suddenly seem bright and full,
Your forever friend gets you through the hard times, the sad
times, and the confused times.

If you turn and walk away, your forever friend follows,
If you lose your way, your forever friend guides you and
cheers you on,
Your forever friend holds your hand and tells you that
everything is going to be okay.

And if you have such a friend,
You feel happy and complete because you need not worry,
You have a forever friend, and forever has no end.

# The Circle of Friendship

We meet online to have a good time,
We laugh and we giggle and smile at our screen,
We sit back and wonder what this could all mean!

We surf the web, we travel afar,
We span thousands of miles without a car,
We watch conversations flowing on the screen,
We tell jokes and stories and know what they mean.

What are we looking for?
What's the attraction?
How can we do this and get satisfaction?
Who are we?
Why are we here?

We are the circle of friends made from a chain,
And we're here because friendship is what we gain!
Born online, formed by few,
We had no idea just what to do.

So we're linking our pages, first one, then two,
And wonder where we'll end up when we're through,
The circle will spread like a wild vine,
It will breathe and whisper like the winds of time.

We are the circle of friends made from a chain,
A chain of cable and wire without an end.

May you have a great time, regardless of where you may be,
There is no friend like an old friend,
Who has shared our morning days,
No greeting like his welcome,
No homage like his praise.

Memories – good or bad – take on a life of their own.

Linda has written hundreds of poems in her life, it's what she does; she doesn't seem to have a choice. Once the pen hits the paper, her emotions, thoughts and fears run free.

Poetry is Linda's way of making sense of the world, of what she sees and feels. Others may pass subjects off as taboo, too uncomfortable to talk about them, but Linda will ride the wave and broach the unthinkable, with no subject out of bounds.

These poems will have you reaching for the tissues, connecting with the most complex of emotions, crying with joy, bellowing with laughter and sobbing with grief and empathy.

Having performed in the pubs of Cambridge, completed radio readings, produced CDs and had her poetry published in greeting cards, Linda's poems have passed through the years like sand through an hourglass.

Linda is a wife, mother, grandma (nan), friend and poet; she will be all of these things forever.

# In My Youth

I remember the corn beef sandwich of my childhood,
And the bread that you could cut with a knife,
When the children did their homework,
And the men went to work, not the wife.
I remember the milk from the bottle,
With the yummy cream on top,
Our dinner came out of the oven,
And not from the freezer or shops.
The kids were a lot more contented,
I didn't need money for kicks,
Just a game with our friends
In the road seemed to do,
And sometimes Saturday night flicks.
I remember the shop on the corner,
And as children we'd try to nick

# Only Me Moaning

I can't walk, my wheelchair is just fine,
I can't lift heavy things, got a husband for that,
I may not do the things you can do
But maybe you can't do the things I can.
The best thing of all I have found is my ability
To not make a big thing of my disability,
But please talk to me when I'm in my chair,
Not the other person there.
I'm a person that would like to relate,
I want you to take stock instead of me
Having to just watch,
I don't want a sad look, I just want you to care,
I am just a person in a chair.
You can ask me what's the matter without a funny look,
You can ask whether I walk at all or even if I can cook,
But don't think that I'm unaware because I'm in a chair,
My legs are just a little heavy; they don't get me anywhere.

# Our Wonderful Queen has Died

Alas, our lovely Queen is dead,
And I hope her soul to heaven has fled,
To sing and rejoice with others around,
Where only joy and peace remain,
And she will meet her husband again.

'Twas September 8th in the evening at 6:22,
When in this world, it was a great shame,
She was surrounded by her children – two of them were there.

She was the model of a very good Queen,
She was very active in her long reign,
She was loved by all throughout the highs
And the lows; the world is devastated,
That she had to go.

The people around Balmoral will shed
Many tears owing to visits over the years,
But in the end, it was her place to rest,
And over Balmoral a rainbow was seen,
For the passing over of our Queen.

I hope they are walking together,
With a happy smile on their faces,
And look at the heather and smell the blossom,
And then they will turn and kiss each other.

They can now look down at their son
With great pride, as the bells ring out
They did hear God save the king,

And they were no more.

# When We Lived Like This

We worked when wages were low,
No telly, no bath, for times were hard,
Just a cold water tap and a pump in the yard,
No holidays abroad, no carpets on floors,
We had coal on the fire and didn't lock doors,
Our children arrived (no pill in those days),
We brought them up without, Ann stated.
Children could just go and play in the park,
And old folk could go out in the dark,
No valium, drugs, and no LSD,
We cured most of our ills with a good cup of tea.
No vandals, no mugging (not much to rob),
We felt we were rich with a couple of bob,
Holidays at home, Sunday School trips,
To the seaside we went and we didn't get sick.
No phones, our friends seemed to be near,
Sometimes mum and dad would go for a beer,
But we seemed to be happy, what else can I say,
I was born in those times and am happy today.
We had hand-me-down clothes and second-hand shoes,
We had ice on our windows in our bedrooms,
We had no fridge or freezer, no central heating

# Paddington the Bear

They had shared tea together that very same day,
When to the palaces he had been invited,
He could hardly speak, he was so excited,
He offered her his most delicious marmalade sandwich.
Alas, Paddington couldn't stand it, he heard it on the news;
His Queen was dead, eighth of September at 6:22,
What could he do?
He sat and cried into his hankey and blew his nose,
He'd heard she'd been a very good Queen for a long time,
Oh, but so upset that she hadn't died in her own bed.
She travelled off to Scotland, Balmoral, her first love,
Surrounded by specialists, her children and grandchildren too,
The people around Balmoral will shed a lot of tears,
Owing to her visits over the years,
But she liked that place the best,
Many happy years she spent at Balmoral smelling the blossoms,
Looking at the greenery and the wonderful heather.
Her husband had always been alongside her,
Holding hands, they'd been happy together with the dogs,
Running, playing in the grounds of her home,
Barking and looking after a real queen.
Well, I must get out of this depression, she's in heaven now,
With her husband, Prince Philip, and all the other kings and
queens
That have died before her, but she is at peace.
Eating his last marmalade sandwich, he smiled –
Heaven must be a wonderful place, he said.

# I Can Just Remember This

I didn't want to remember.
Children, shivering and shaking like the wind,
Mothers, searching for a piece of stale bread,
Shadows on thin legs moving with fear;
No, we didn't want to remember any of this,
Families that moved and vanished during the night,
Fleeing for their safety.

The mass graves, the smell of death, the smoke,
Pile the bodies and pile them high,
Make them a mountain up to the sky,
Toss them and turn them and keep them as well,
It will not hurt them, they're all going to hell.
The bodies are useless; the souls will be set free,
But stories are fixed in their glassy-grained eyes,
And we can still feel the pain that's hidden inside.

Every time I write something like this,
I feel so desperately sad for what went on during wartime,
I can easily cry things I write for all this,
So they just gave their lives for us,
And then sometimes I look around at the world and think,
"What are we giving back? Looked at a football match the
other week; That's just one thing,"
This world, it's for the next generation and the one after that,
So please, let's try to get it right,
No killing policemen or anyone for that matter,

Well, that poor politician,
July 2022
View Image
So maybe tonight we can say a short prayer
For the people we love and have lost.

# Transgender I wish

The body I was given is not the one I want or wish to own,
This cursed horrid body seeks my deepest phobia,
I want to cut off my hair, I want people to see I am a boy.
I am in the wrong body, I can cry, I can scream, I can shout,
I will never give up,
But I want the world to understand I don't know pretty dresses,
No makeup, push-up bras or holding in knickers – oh no, I'm
a boy.
I haven't got stubble, and I haven't got a beard,
I know I've got a body part that I'd rather weren't there,
But I've heard that if I save up, it can be changed, so that's
not bad,
It's better that I do this than sit around and just be sad.
The top half didn't grow much, flat-chested people say,
But I'd rather have them like that than big ones that get in
the way,
But I think I'm going to think a bit, I do have a lot of time,
I'll go in and have my tea, you see, I'm only 9!

# The Old Man

*A grey-haired old man who lives by himself,*
*Just watching the time pass by,*
He analyses the years going by,
He wonders why it went too fast.
He should have smiled once in a while,
A few hours of his time to enjoy life for a while,
But he watched himself fading away,
And he had other thoughts on his mind.
His mistakes, misadventures and opportunities,
He slowly began to unwind,
He realised he wasn't a good man,
He hadn't done a lot with his life.
He treated his wife quite badly,
She wanted children and he wouldn't oblige,
But now he was ready for this commitment,
So he planned a romantic evening for two.
His wife was very confused, this had never happened before,
So she dressed herself up in her Sunday best,
"You look nice," he said,
"Tell me, where are we going?"
"To the pub," he said, "It will be nice,
Then I'll drag you to bed to make babies, like you said,
I've had a change of mind,"
"Don't bother, I'm 55."